Fun STEM Challenges

BUILDING STRONG BRIDGES

by Marne Ventura

PEBBLE
a capstone imprint

Pebble Plus is published by Pebble, an imprint of Capstone.
1710 Roe Crest Drive, North Mankato, Minnesota 56003
www.capstonepub.com

Library of Congress Cataloging-in-Publication data is available on the Library of Congress website.
ISBN: 978-1-9771-1299-6 (library binding)
ISBN: 978-1-9771-1779-3 (paperback)
ISBN: 978-1-9771-1305-4 (ebook pdf)

Summary: Describes why bridges are useful as well as how to make and test bridges made out of paper.

Image Credits
Photographs by Capstone: Karon Dubke;
Marcy Morin and Sarah Schuette, project production;
Heidi Thompson, art director

Shutterstock: Brandon Seidel, 7, Jess Kraft, 1, Miroslava Durcatova, 5

All the rest of the images are credited to: Capstone Studio/Karon Dubke

Editorial Credits
Erika L. Shores, editor; Juliette Peters, designer;
Eric Gohl, media researcher;
Laura Manthe, production specialist

All internet sites appearing in back matter were available and accurate when this book was sent to press.

Capstone thanks Darsa Donelan, Ph.D., assistant professor of physics, Gustavus Adolphus College, St. Peter, MN, for her expertise in reviewing this book.

Printed in China.
2493

Table of Contents

What Is a Bridge? 4

Why Build Bridges? 6

Make Your Own........................ 8

Test It.................................. 18

What Did You Learn? 20

Glossary 22

Read More...............................23

Internet Sites 23

Critical Thinking Questions.........24

Index....................................24

What Is a Bridge?

Bridges join places together.

They go over rivers and valleys.

Why Build Bridges?

Bridges let us get across.

They carry roads over water.

Without a bridge, a road
would end at the edge of the water.

Make Your Own

You can make a bridge with many things. Use wood blocks and thick paper. Gather some toy cars too. What else could you use for a bridge?

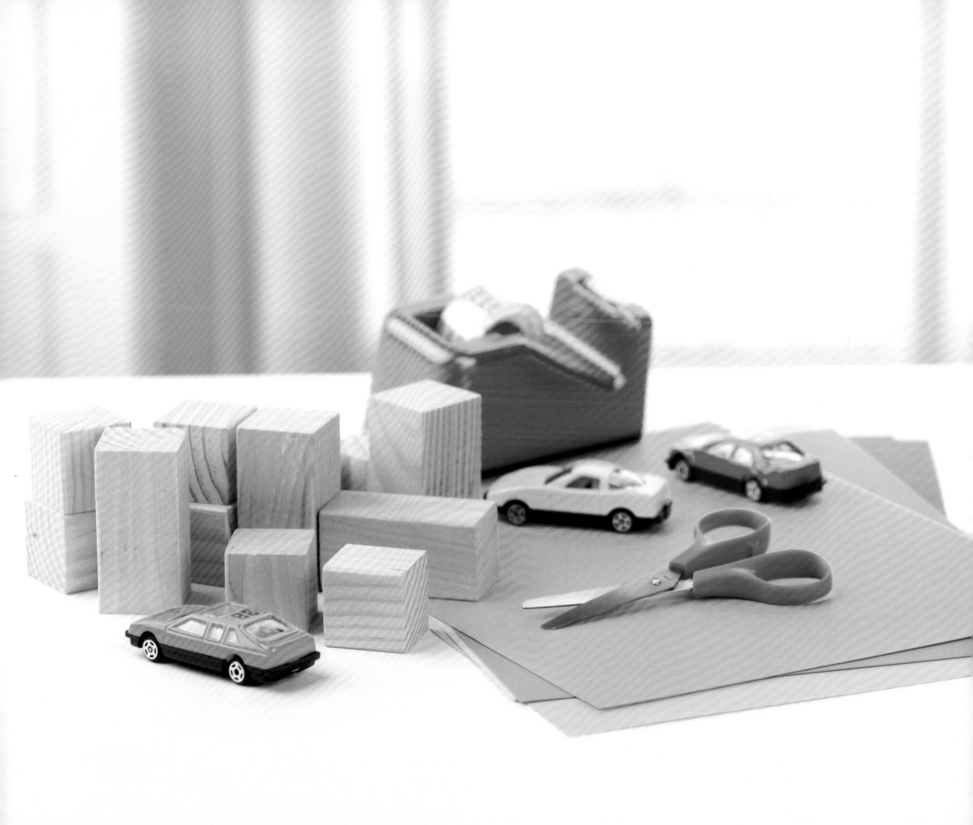

Cars drive over bridge beams.

Make a beam bridge with thick paper.

Blocks hold up the paper beam.

They carry the weight of the beam

and the cars on the bridge.

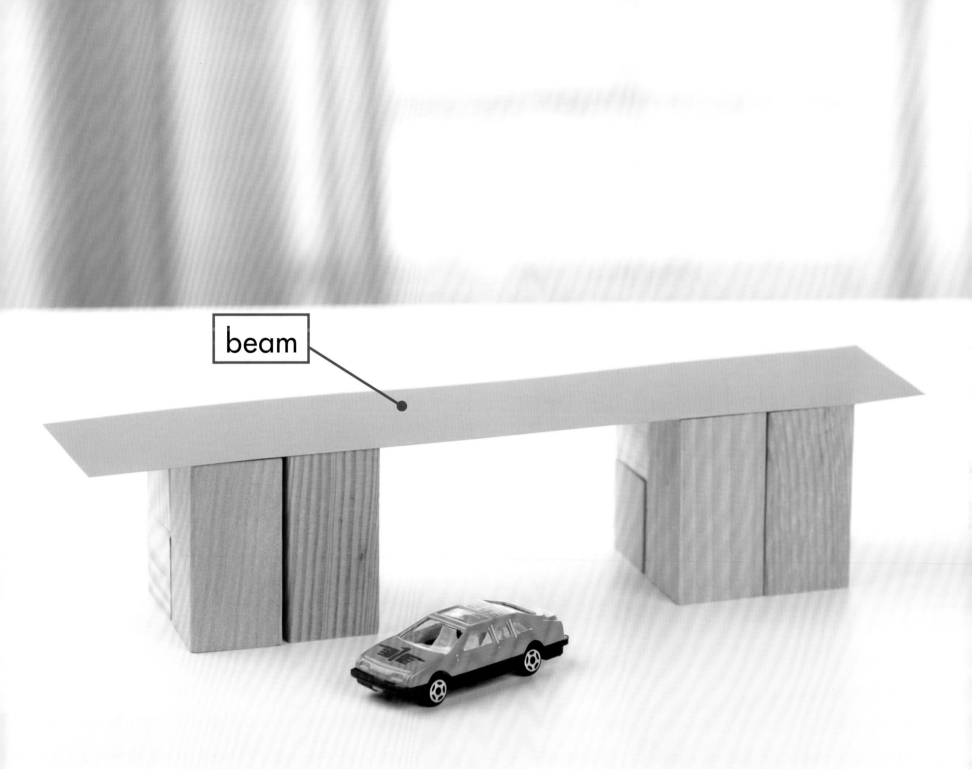

beam

A long bridge needs more than end blocks to hold it up. It needs support in the middle. The middle blocks help hold up the beam.

support

13

An arch is a strong shape.

It carries the weight from

the beam and cars to the blocks.

Try holding up the beam

with a paper arch.

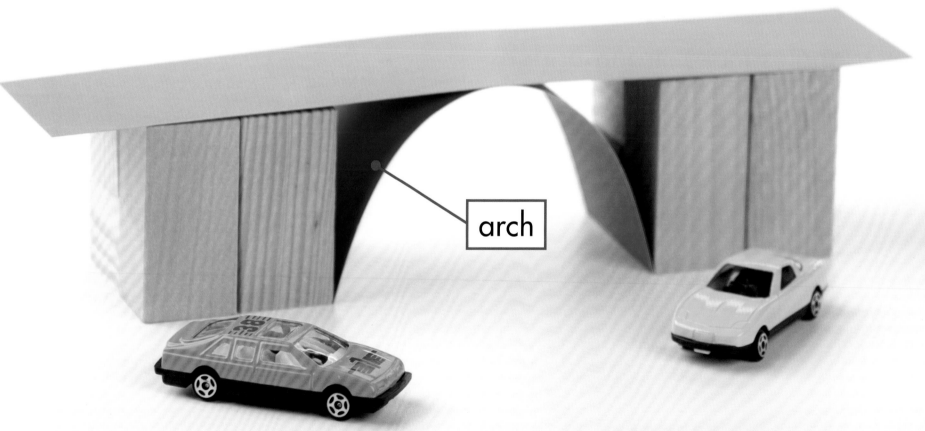

arch

A triangle is a strong shape.

Some bridges use triangles for support.

Triangles make strong bridges.

Fold thick paper like a fan.

See the triangles?

Test It

How many cars will each bridge hold?

Which bridge is strongest?

Does a long beam need

more support than a short beam?

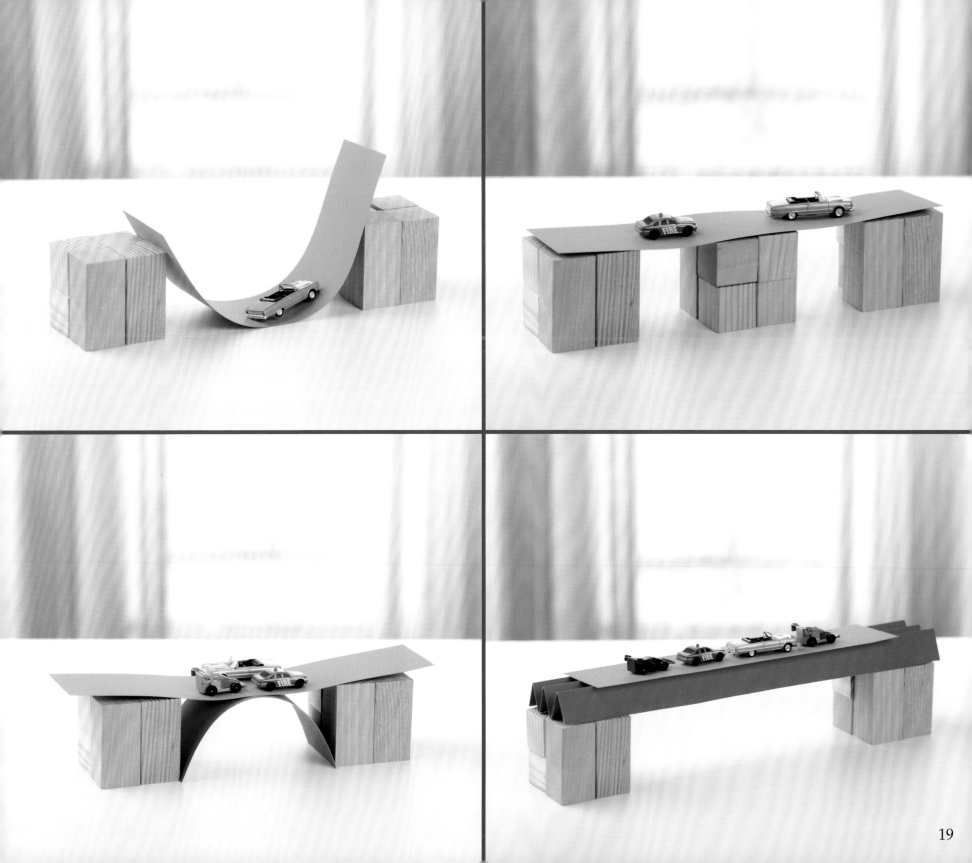

What Did You Learn?

End posts hold up bridge beams.

Middle posts support long bridges.

Arches and triangles are

strong shapes for bridges.

Glossary

arch—a curved shape

beam—a long straight piece of material such as wood or metal

post—a piece of metal or wood placed firmly in an upright position and used especially as a support to hold up something

support—to hold the weight of an object

triangle—a figure with three sides and three angles

Read More

Bell, Samantha S. *Building Bridges.* Lake Elmo, MN: Focus Readers, 2018.

Enz, Tammy. *Building Bridges.* Chicago: Heinemann Raintree, 2017.

Isbell, Hannah. *Zoom in on Bridges.* New York: Enslow Publishing, 2018.

Internet Sites

Bridge Basics
http://www.pbs.org/wgbh/buildingbig/bridge/basics.html

Build a Bridge
https://www.pbs.org/wgbh/nova/bridge/build.html

Critical Thinking Questions

1. Why do bridges need to be strong?

2. Why do bridges need arches?

3. How do bridges help us?

Index

arches, 14, 20
beams, 10, 12, 14, 18, 20
blocks, 8, 10, 12, 14
cars, 8, 10, 14, 18
paper, 8, 10, 14, 16
posts, 20

rivers, 4
roads, 6
support, 12, 16, 18, 20
triangles, 16, 20
valleys, 4
weight, 10, 14